YOUR KNOWLEDGE HAS VALUE

- We will publish your bachelor's and
  master's thesis, essays and papers

- Your own eBook and book -
  sold worldwide in all relevant shops

- Earn money with each sale

Upload your text at www.GRIN.com
and publish for free

Bibliographic information published by the German National Library:

The German National Library lists this publication in the National Bibliography; detailed bibliographic data are available on the Internet at http://dnb.dnb.de .

This book is copyright material and must not be copied, reproduced, transferred, distributed, leased, licensed or publicly performed or used in any way except as specifically permitted in writing by the publishers, as allowed under the terms and conditions under which it was purchased or as strictly permitted by applicable copyright law. Any unauthorized distribution or use of this text may be a direct infringement of the author s and publisher s rights and those responsible may be liable in law accordingly.

Imprint:

Copyright © 2015 GRIN Verlag
Print and binding: Books on Demand GmbH, Norderstedt Germany
ISBN: 9783668951129

This book at GRIN:

https://www.grin.com/document/470310

Alfredo Lopez

Digital Forensics Tools and Techniques

GRIN Verlag

GRIN - Your knowledge has value

Since its foundation in 1998, GRIN has specialized in publishing academic texts by students, college teachers and other academics as e-book and printed book. The website www.grin.com is an ideal platform for presenting term papers, final papers, scientific essays, dissertations and specialist books.

Visit us on the internet:

http://www.grin.com/

http://www.facebook.com/grincom

http://www.twitter.com/grin_com

Digital Forensics Tools and Techniques

By

Alfredo Lopez

2015

1.0- Introduction

Nowadays the use of computers is increasing more and more. This has allowed the development of the internet. In turn, the Internet has brought many benefits, but the internet has also contributed to the rise of cyber-crime. So, with the rise of cybercrime, it has become critical to increase and develop computer systems security.

Each time, the techniques used by cybercriminals are more sophisticated, making it more difficult to protect corporate networks. Because of this, the computer security of these companies has been violated, and it is here at this point when digital analysis forensic is needed to discover cybercriminals.

So, with the rise of cybercrime, digital forensics is increasingly gaining importance in the area of information technology. For this reason, when a crime is done, the crime information is stored digitally. Therefore, it must use appropriate mechanisms for the collection, preservation, protection, analysis and presentation of digital evidence stored in electronic devices. It is here that the need arises for digital forensics.

In this report, I am going to explain what digital forensics is. Also, I will describe some forensic software and hardware and the importance of suitable forensic labs. So, let's start.

2.0- What is Digital Forensics?

Digital Forensics is IT (Information Technology) specialization that assumes the necessary duties related with finding exhibit (evidence) at the place where a crime has been committed (crime scene) Digital forensic duties include: identify, collect, preserve, analysis, interpret, document and present evidence. This implies that those involved in this new and necessary discipline must be professionals with high ethical standards and respect for institutions, for in them is support decisions on the events analysed (National Institute of Justice, 2010).

Forensic investigators have professional tools and techniques that help them recreate what happened with a computer or other electronic device. Thanks to these techniques' researchers can discover how a computer was used to commit a crime. Two of these techniques are:

    1- Determine who used the computer? How was used? When and why?
        ---The recovery of deleted files
        ---Elemental Decryption
        ---Search different types of files
        ---Search a certain process

2- Determine who has a remote user on the computer from someone else?
---Read log files
---Rebuild actions
---Tracing the origin

2.1- What is Digital Evidence?

Any document, file, record, data, etc. Content or electronically stored, for example:

--Office documents (Word, Excel, Power point)
--Digital Communication (E-mail)
--Digital images (photos and videos)
--Databases
--File activity logs (Logs)

Digital evidence can be found in the following devices:
--Hard Drives
--Cell phones
-- (PDA) Personal digital assistants
-- DVDs CDs &
--Memory cards and other storage devices
(National Institute of Justice, 2010).

2. 2- Phases of the digital forensics process

The phases of the digital forensic process are: Protect the crime scene, collect the evidence, and establish the chain of custody and examination of the evidence.

- **Secure the crime scene:**
  Securing the crime scene (the place where a crime has been committed) involves protecting evidence that can be found in the scene. If the scene is not properly secured, then the evidence could be contaminated. For them, basic techniques to secure the crime scene are:

  - Keep out unauthorized personnel to the scene
  - Look carefully all the details in the scene
  - Do not touch anything. If the suspect computer is on, then do not turn it off. Do not click with the mouse or pressing any key on the keyboard. If the suspect computer is off, then, do not turn it on. (If it is necessary to turn off the computer, the power cable must be pulled off from the back of the computer)
  - Take photos of all the relevant details to the case
  - Write down all the details in a notebook

- **Collect the evidence:**
  This step includes collecting physical and digital evidence. For example, we can take photos of how a suspect computer is connected and what peripherals have connected. This information can be used as physical evidence. On the other hand, extract the data stored in the hard drive disk or in the RAM memory of the computer, is collect digital evidence.

- **Establish a chain of custody:**
  The chain of custody is the life cycle of evidence. This life cycle starts from the time of evidence collection until the final report and result of the case. The chain of custody allows ensures the integrity and protection of the specimen. Therefore, is very important to keep a record of all operations performed on the chain of custody.

- **Evidence examination:**
  Evidence examination involves those tasks oriented to locate and extract digital evidence relevant to the investigation by applying various techniques and forensic tools that attempt to respond to the points required by the client. So, in the next chapters, I will show these necessary forensic tools to examine digital evidence (Ciampa, 2012).

3.0 - Digital Forensic Software Tools

As I have before mentioned, digital forensics science has several steps required to complete an investigation. These stages are: securing the crime scene, acquisition, analysis and presentation of evidence. To perform the aforementioned is required to use professional techniques and suitable forensic tools that allow the acquisition of images of hard disks for later analysis and presentation of the results. Therefore, I will describe some digital forensic tools that permit to achieve the objectives above described.

3.1- The Sleuth Kit and Autopsy:

This is a kit of commands lines for system analysis. This valuable forensic software helps us to navigate through the files from the suspect computer without altering anything on this computer. In addition, this forensic tool like many others is able to show us a detailed list of deleted files and hidden files. It also supports various types of partitions such as sun, Mac, BSD, DOS and others. This helps us to identify certain partitions in particular to find digital evidence. However, a disadvantage of this forensic tool is that you must to memorize all commands, and it is tedious but is here in this part when Autopsy can help.

Autopsy is a forensic tool with a graphical user interface and browser to analysis evidence. Autopsy can analysis different types of data format such as FAT, Ext2 / Ext3, NTFS, etc. Autopsy is Open Source and can run on UNIX platforms. Also, we can install and runs autopsy on Windows environments. Autopsy is based on HTML, So, this feature permits the connection with the server of Autopsy employing a web browser. Also, deleted files and data are shown by an interface of Autopsy called "File Manager". For these reasons, Autopsy is a very popular forensic tool to find evidence (Autopsy, 2013-2015).

3.2- ProDiscover Basic:

ProDiscover Basic is a free digital forensic tool that like Autopsy has a graphical user interface. This forensic tool is designed to make copies of the hard disk without altering any data on this. ProDiscover Basic also permits to create images of USB flash memory, RAM memory images, BIOS image and hard drives images. Once the image is ready, we can analyse in detail the evidence found for this wonderful software. Some features of this digital forensic tool are:

- View Deleted files
- Search for contents of a disk
- Retrieve a file that was accidentally deleted
- Registry view
- Event log view
- Internet history view
- View logs
- Hashing MD5, SHA1 & SHA256
- Auto verify image Checksum
- Signature analysis
- Forensic report

  I can personally say that I really like the report generated by ProDiscover Basic. This report is very comprehensive and detailed. I strongly believe that this software produces better reports that the reports made by Autopsy. In My view, the reports from Autopsy are very poor (ProDiscover Basic, 2015).

3.3- EnCase Enterprise:

According to the website of the provider, Encase contributes advanced forensic analysis tool for digital investigation. EnCase is an instinctive tool that has a useful user interface and amazing performance. EnCase forensic supplies all the necessary for vast stopover digital analysis in deep investigations with accuracy and safety. An award-triumphant software that ensures the full integrity of the information processed allowing easy manage of vast volumes of digital evidence, even deleted data, in areas of slack, paging areas and unallocated clusters files. Some features of this forensic tool are:

- Support for multiple images systems such as Linux, Windows, MAC OS, Solaris, HP UX.
- Full Support for Unicode

- The ability of multiple systems analysis
- Search tools
- Allow the use of RAID 0,1 & 5
- Support for compressed NTFS File Systems
- Gets data from disk or RAM, documents, pictures, email, web mail, Internet appliances, cache and web history, reconstruction of HTML websites, chat sessions, archives, backup files, and encrypted files.

According to the provider's website says that "due to its powerful and efficient functions, EnCase Enterprise has become the standard reliable solution for digital investigations. No other product offers the same level of functionality, acceptance and performance" (EnCase Forensic, 1997).

3.4- DEFT:

DEFT (Digital Evidence and Forensic Toolkit) is a distribution of Linux based on Xubuntu 9.10 with kernel 2.6.31, LXDE desktop along with a GUI for forensic applications. DEFT is designed to police, researchers, system administrators or forensic specialists. The first edition of DEFT was launched in 2005 at the University of Bologna Italy on a computer forensics competition conducted by the Faculty of Law. Since then DEFT has been gaining ground as a forensic tool kit. This Linux distribution is free and can be downloaded from the Internet and used as a Live CD or USB memory.

DEFT is a useful forensic tool because it is able to provide accurate and reliable analysis to forensic investigators, and this is because DEFT ensures the integrity of data structures and metadata in the system that is being analyzed without altering the data. When the system is booting, the partition in the system that must be analysed is not touched by DFET to make any changes. This allows the integrity of the system without alteration of the system files. DEFT has many applications, which will describe below (DEFT, 2015).

Sleuthkit 3.2.3	libewf 20120304	hex dump	iPhone backup analyzer
autopsy 2.24	aff lib 3.6.14	outguess 0.2	phone analyzer
dff 1.2	Disk Utility 2.30.1	Sqlite database browser 2.0b1	creepy 0.1.9
ptk forensic 1.0.5	guymager 0.6.5	bitpim 1.0.7	xprobe2 0.3
Maltego CE	dd rescue 1.14	bbwhatsapp database	xmount 0.4.6trlD 2.11 DEFT Edition
KeepNote 0.7.6	dcfldd 1.3.4.1	converter	readpst 0.6.41
hunchbackeed file carver 0.6	dc3dd 7	Dropbox reader	chkrootkit

Findwild 1.3	foremost 1.5.6	md5sum	rkhunter 1.3.8
Bulk Extractor 1.2	photorec 6.13	sha1sum	john 1.7.8
Emule F	mount manager 0.2.6	sha224sum	pasco 1.0
orensic 1.0	scalpel 2	sha256sum	Wireshark 1.6
dhash 2.0.1	Wipe 0.2	catfish	mobius forensic

3.5- Internet Evidence Finder:

Internet Evidence Finder is a software tool that enables the recovery of data that has been deleted or that are currently stored on the hard drive, as a result of communications right through the internet. This means that Internet Evidence Finder can recover all types of social networks data, such as popular web mail applications, browsing the history, chat histories instant messaging, and other online communications.

According to the creators of this software, Internet Evidence Finder is able to retrieve much more data than other similar software. The truth is that this forensic tool is very useful when it comes to search for keywords or blocks of words related to an investigation where the Internet was used to commit any crime. When the internet or any social network have been used to commit a crime, Internet Evidence Finder may help us discover the attacker. For example, nowadays is very common that many attackers use fake Facebook accounts to commit crimes, but Internet Evidence Finder can help us discover who is behind these fake accounts of Facebook and other social networks (Internet Evidence Finder, 2014).

4.0- Digital Forensic Hardware Tools

In the previous chapter, I mentioned several digital forensic software tools that can be used to find evidence and find those who commit cybercrimes. But all those forensic software tools are not useful if you do not have the suitable hardware to run all those forensic applications. For this reason, in chapter 4, I will describe some digital forensic hardware tools necessary for forensic investigation.

4.1- FRED (Forensic Recovery of Evidence Device)

This is a powerful forensic computer and is very useful for use in the laboratory. This workstation has been created for the acquisition and analysis of digital evidence. FRED has removable trays for connecting multiple hard drives. Thus, the forensic investigator only has to remove the hard drive from the suspect computer and insert it into one of the removable trays provided by FRED to start looking for digital evidence. This forensic computer tolerate different types of hard drives, such as IDE disks, SATA, ATA, EIDE, SAS, ATAPI, Firewire, USB drives and other devices for storing the which we can find digital evidence such as CDs, DVDs, Blu-Ray, Secure Multimedia Card, XD Cards, Memory Stick, Smart Media, Micro Drives, Compact Flash and many others. As if that were not enough, FRED comes with optional tape drives, which allows us to archive and \ or acquire evidence from LTO Ultrium 5 tape. Another nice feature of FRED is that thanks to its front panel connections for connecting hard drives, we do not need to open the computer to connect the hard drives (FRED, 2015).

4.2- Talon Enhanced

This is a portable device that allows forensic copying hard drives at a speed of more than 7GB / min, without altering or modifying files stored on these hard drives. This forensic tool has been specially designed for the fieldwork due to its portability but also can be used in the forensic laboratory. In the field when the digital forensic investigator is on the crime-scene, he can remove the hard drive from the suspect computer and connect it to Talon Enhanced to start copying the hard-suspect disk. Some features of this forensic hardware are:

- Ruggedized, scratch-resistant exterior and impact resistant display.
- Compact, lightweight, and portable.
- Provides 100% write protection
- Capture to multiple image formats
- Compatible with different forensic analysis software
- Capture from 1 suspect to 1 or 2 evidence drives at speeds over 7GB/min
- Support for IDE/SATA drives is built into the Talon Enhanced. Support for SCSI, SAS, and micro SATA drives
- Uses the highest level of authentication MD5 and SHA256 hash

(Talon Enhanced, 2015)

4.3- Celldek Tek

CELLDEK Tek is a forensic device tool that allows you to retrieve evidence from cell phones and personal digital assistants (PDA). This forensic hardware is portable, allowing the forensic field work, but can also be used in the forensic laboratory. This forensic tool supports more than 950 types of mobile phones and is able to quickly obtain and extract digital evidence of these phones. As already mentioned, CELLDEK Tek is a valuable tool for digital forensic investigators who need to seek evidence in suspected phones. Additionally, this hardware has a touch screen that provides detailed information about the suspect phone, such as the phone model, brand, serial, dimensions (Celldek Tek, 2015).

Features:

- Data Extraction
- Data Acquiring
- Image Download
- Audit Trail
- Auto-select Adapter Cables
- Backup Archive
- Data Format
- Cable System
- MD5 Hash
- Read/Write Features
  Ports toggled from read-only to write-only
- PDA Compatible
  Acquires all files and data from Windows PDA's
- Reports
  Provides HTML reports

4.4- Forensic Dossier

This hardware tool is designed exclusively for forensic data capture, the Forensic Dossier is the sixth generation of forensic solutions Logicube. Forensic Dossier is equipped with the latest technology along with a user-friendly interface. Some of its features are:

- Perfect for the field and laboratory
- Capable of offering simultaneous capture 1 or 2 discs objective 1 or 2 discs of evidence
- Native support for SATA and IDE devices and USB and Firewire
- Speeds up to 7GB / min
- Supports acquisition E01 supports EnCase and FTK format v3.x
- Optional support for SCSI and SAS devices
- Authentication MD5 and SHA
- Device Support 2TB NTFS and more
- Ability to capture a greater goal 2 smaller devices
- Advanced Search Keywords
- Compatible with MPFS
- Capture HPA and DCO
- Integrated QWERTY keyboard
- Optional module for access via a network (Forensic Dossier, 2014).

4.5- SHADOW 3

This hardware is designed to help forensic to access the magnetic media without changing the content investigators. Main features are:

- Allows investigating hard drives in the crime-scene within minutes, before creating the image. With the steady increase in capacity of hard disks, saving time when prioritizing the order of the disks to the image, or even eliminate the need to create the image of certain disks when it is a multiple capture.

- Allows investigate and analyze source discs and again in the forensic laboratory in seconds without having to recreate the image.

- Allows viewing the evidence in their native environment.

- Allows present evidence in an understandable way for non-experts in the computer itself investigated.

- When a suspected illegal activity, such as nighttime download sensitive files, use Shadow to verify activity and preserve the metadata (Shadow 3, 2015).

5.0 - Forensic LABS

So far, we have analysed the two types of forensic tools to find digital evidence and catch those who commit computer crimes. These two types of tool that we have analysed are forensic software and hardware. Both combined tools provide valuable assistance to a digital forensic investigator. However, these two already mentioned tools also need a forensic laboratory. This is because not all the forensic work can be performed in the field, you need a laboratory to perform a more thorough forensic investigation.

Depending on the size of a forensic company, we can design the ideal laboratory. The forensic laboratory must be able to have the necessary hardware and software as we have described throughout this report. Moreover, depending on the circumstances, a forensic laboratory may be small, medium or large. Digital forensic laboratory facilities should generally be divided into at least three parts, which will describe below.

- **Mechanical Room:**
  In this area, computers are disassembled if necessary. Hard drives and RAM memories can be removed.

- **Storage Room:**
  In this area, all the evidence found is stored. Including the chain of custody.

- **Analysis Room:**
  This is the most important area of the digital forensics lab because there is where all suspicious computers are analysed to find evidence that may incriminate those responsible people.

Some larger forensic laboratories can be divided as follows:

- Reception room
- Mechanical room
- Evidence room or Storage room
- Analysis rooms
- Offices
- Library
- Conference room

(Nelson, Phillips & Steuart, 2010).

6.0- Conclusion and recommendations

Throughout this report, I have described the importance of digital forensic science. We have seen, that this digital science, is a branch of computer system security. The computer system security is applied to prevent cybercriminals from stealing data from businesses. But when the computer system security has failed and a cyber-crime has been committed, then this is where the other part of the computer system security now known as digital forensics science enters. This science uses tools and techniques to capture, preserve, protect and present digital data that can incriminate the responsible to commit cyber-crimes.

In this report, on chapter two I have explained that Digital Forensics is IT specialization that assumes the necessary duties related of finding exhibit (evidence) at the place where a crime has been committed (crime scene) their duties include: identify, collect, preserve, analysis, interpret, document and present evidence. On chapter three I showed five Digital Forensic Software Tools such as The Sleuth Kit and Autopsy, ProDiscover Basic, EnCase Enterprise, DEFT and Internet Evidence Finder. On chapter four, I described five forensic hardware such as FRED (Forensic Recovery of Evidence Device), Talon Enhanced, Celldek Tek, Forensic Dossier and SHADOW 3. Finally, in chapter five I have talked, about the suitable of forensic laboratories.

As we have seen in this report, there are many digital forensic tools. So, my recommendation is that we can use the most appropriate forensic tool for a specific case. Each forensic tool has its advantages and disadvantages, for example, I like working with Autopsy, but I much prefer the reports generated by ProDiscover Basic, because the reports from Autopsy are very poor. I recommend that everyone use the digital forensic tool that you like and that know how to use successfully.

There is no doubt that with the increase of cyber-crimes, digital forensics science will continue to grow in the coming years.

7.0- References

Autopsy. (2003-2015). Retrieved from:

> http://www.sleuthkit.org/autopsy/index.php

Celldek Tek. (2015). Retrieved from:

> http://www.logicube.com/knowledge/celldek-tek

Ciampa, M. (2012). *Security+ Guide to Network Security Fundamentals.* (4th Ed.). Boston, United States: Cengage Learning.

DEFT. (2015). Retrieved from:

> http://www.deftlinux.net/

EnCase Forensic. (1997). Retrieved from:

> https://www.guidancesoftware.com/products/Pages/encase-forensic/overview.aspx

Forensic Dossier. (2014). Retrieved from:
> http://www.logicube.com/shop/forensic-dossier/

FRED. (2015). Retrieved form:
> http://www.digitalintelligence.com/products/fred/

Internet Evidence Finder. (2014). Retrieved from:

> https://www.fbo.gov/index?s=opportunity&mode=form&id=2d7a580af47a91ea37a7a2cf320a24fd&tab=core&_cview=1

National Institute of Justice. (2010). Retrieved from:

> http://nij.gov/topics/forensics/evidence/digital/pages/welcome.aspx

Nelson, B., Phillips, A. & Steuart, C. (2010). *Guide to computer forensics and investigations* (4th Ed.). Boston, United States: Cengage Learning.

ProDiscover Basic. (2015). Retrieved from:

> http://prodiscover-basic.software.informer.com/

SHADOW 3. (2015). Retrieved from:

    http://www.digitalintelligence.com/products/shadow3

Talon Enhanced. (2015). Retrieved from:

    http://www.logicube.com/shop/talon-enhanced/

YOUR KNOWLEDGE HAS VALUE

- We will publish your bachelor's and master's thesis, essays and papers

- Your own eBook and book -
  sold worldwide in all relevant shops

- Earn money with each sale

Upload your text at www.GRIN.com
and publish for free